step-by-step

one pot

p

This is a Parragon Book
First published in 2002

Parragon
Queen Street House
4 Queen Street
Bath BA1 1HE, UK

ISBN: 0-75258-005-1

Printed in Spain

Produced by The Bridgewater Book Company Ltd, Lewes, East Sussex

Acknowledgements
Creative Director Terry Jeavons
Art Director Sarah Howerd
Editorial Director Fiona Biggs
Senior Editor Mark Truman
Editorial Assistants Simon Bailey, Tom Kitch
Page Make-up Sara Kidd

NOTES FOR THE READER

- This book uses both metric and imperial measurements. Follow the same units of measurement throughout; do not mix metric and imperial.
- All spoon measurements are level: teaspoons are assumed to be 5 ml, and table-spoons are assumed to be 15 ml.
- Unless otherwise stated, milk is assumed to be full-fat, eggs and individual vegetables such as potatoes are medium-sized, and pepper is freshly ground black pepper.
- Recipes using raw or very lightly cooked eggs should be avoided by infants, the elderly, pregnant women, convalescents, and anyone suffering from an illness.
- Optional ingredients, variations, and serving suggestions have not been included in the calculations.
- The times given are an approximate guide only. Preparation times differ according to the techniques used by different people, and the cooking times vary as a result of the type of oven used.

Contents

Introduction

A collection of delicious recipes which are really easy to prepare and cook is a boon for anyone who has little time to spend in the kitchen or who needs an idea for a filling dish that can be prepared in minutes. All the dishes in this book are substantial enough to make a meal. They range from thick soups, such as Spicy Lamb Soup with Chickpeas & Courgettes, bursting with hearty ingredients, such as Golden Chicken Risotto and Chinese Fried Rice, which make wonderful main meals. They include some new and exciting ideas, and recipes for vegetarians Cashew Nut Paella and Spiced Lentils with Spinach. All can be cooked in one pot, so there is no juggling with half-a-dozen pans, and no huge pile of washing up afterwards.

Choose the right recipe, and half an hour after returning home from work you could be sitting down to a delicious Seafood Stew

guide to recipe key	
very easy	Recipes are graded as follows: 1 pea = easy; 2 peas = very easy; 3 peas = extremely easy.
makes 24	Recipes generally serve four people. Simply halve the ingredients to serve two, taking care not to mix imperial and metric measurements.
15 minutes	Preparation time. Where marinating or soaking noodles are involved, these times have been added on separately: eg, 15 minutes + 30 minutes to marinate.
15 minutes	Cooking time. Cooking times don't include the cooking of rice or noodles served with the main dishes.

or Chinese Fried Rice. Alternatively, you could throw the ingredients for a Lamb Hotpot or a Chickpea & Vegetable Casserole into a pot, then relax in the bath, or catch up with friends while it cooks. Baked Tomato Rice with Sausages takes only 15 minutes to prepare, and the dish is tasty and filling.

One-pot meals eliminate hours of preparation and cooking for guests. A menu of Oriental Pork Balls & Greens in Broth followed by Spicy Coconut Rice with Monkfish & Peas and Osso Bucco with Citrus Rinds, makes stylish dinner party fare for friends.

Stir-fried Squid with Hot Black Bean Sauce, page 62

Soups & Starters

The recipes in this section need a minimum of preparation. The ingredients of these soups do not need to be cooked separately, then blended together in a liquidizer or a food processor before reheating. Instead meat, vegetables, beans and grains are all cooked together. Served with hunks of bread, each soup makes a complete meal. Beef Goulash Soup makes a filling lunch or evening meal. Vegetable Chilli and Vegetable Soup with Bulgar Wheat & Herbs were both created with vegetarians in mind.

Beef Goulash Soup

1 tbsp oil
500 g/1 lb 2 oz lean
   minced beef
2 onions, chopped finely
2 garlic cloves, chopped
   finely
2 tbsp plain flour
225 ml/8 fl oz water
400 g/14 oz canned
   chopped tomatoes
   in juice
1 carrot, chopped finely
225 g/8 oz red pepper,
   roasted, peeled,
   de-seeded and
   chopped
1 tsp Hungarian paprika
¼ tsp caraway seeds
pinch of dried oregano
1 litre/1¾ pints beef
   stock
60 g/2¼ oz tagliatelle,
   broken into small
   pieces
salt and pepper
soured cream and fresh
   coriander, to garnish

❶ Heat the oil in a large wide saucepan over a medium–high heat. Add the beef and sprinkle with salt and pepper. Fry until lightly browned.

❷ Reduce the heat and add the onions and garlic. Fry for about 3 minutes, stirring frequently, until the onions are softened. Stir in the flour and continue cooking the beef and onions for 1 minute.

❸ Add the water and stir to combine well, scraping the bottom of the pan to mix in the flour. Stir in the tomatoes, carrot, pepper, paprika, caraway seeds, oregano and stock.

❹ Bring just to the boil. Reduce the heat, cover and simmer gently for about 40 minutes, stirring occasionally, until all the vegetables are tender.

❺ Add the tagliatelle to the soup and simmer for another 20 minutes, or until the pasta is cooked.

❻ Taste the soup and adjust the seasoning, if necessary. Ladle into warm bowls and top each with a tablespoon of soured cream. Garnish with coriander.

extremely easy

serves 4

10 minutes

1 hour,
20 minutes

Chinese Pork Balls & Greens in Broth

INGREDIENTS

2 litres/3½ pints chicken
    stock
85 g/3 oz shiitake
    mushrooms, sliced
    thinly
175 g/6 oz pak choi or
    other Eastern greens,
    sliced into thin
    ribbons
6 spring onions,
    sliced finely
salt and pepper

PORK BALLS
225 g/8 oz lean minced
    pork
25 g/1 oz fresh spinach
    leaves, chopped finely
2 spring onions,
    chopped finely
1 garlic clove, chopped
    very finely
pinch of Chinese 5-spice
    powder
1 tsp soy sauce

❶ To make the pork balls, put the pork, spinach, spring onions and garlic in a bowl. Add the 5-spice powder and soy sauce, and mix until combined.

❷ Shape the pork mixture into 24 balls. Place them in one layer in a steamer that will fit over the top of a saucepan.

❸ Bring the stock just to the boil in a saucepan that will accommodate the steamer. Regulate the heat so that the liquid bubbles gently. Add the mushrooms to the stock and place the steamer, covered, on top of the pan. Steam for 10 minutes. Remove the steamer and set aside on a plate.

❹ Add the pak choi or greens and spring onions to the pan, and cook gently in the stock for 3–4 minutes, or until the leaves are wilted. Taste the soup and adjust the seasoning, if necessary, to taste.

❺ Divide the pork balls evenly among 6 warm bowls and ladle the soup over them. Serve at once.

very easy

serves 6

15 minutes

25–30 minutes

Spicy Lamb Soup with Chickpeas & Courgettes

INGREDIENTS

1–2 tbsp olive oil
450 g/1 lb lean boneless
   lamb, such as shoulder
   or neck fillet, trimmed
   of fat and cut into
   1 cm/ ½ inch cubes
1 onion, chopped finely
2–3 garlic cloves, crushed
1.2 litres/2 pints water
400 g/14 oz canned
   chopped tomatoes
   in juice
1 bay leaf
½ tsp dried thyme
½ tsp dried oregano
⅛ tsp ground cinnamon
¼ tsp ground cumin
¼ tsp ground turmeric
1 tsp harissa, or more
   to taste
400 g/14 oz canned
   chickpeas, drained
   and rinsed
1 carrot, diced
1 potato, diced
1 courgette, quartered
   lengthways and sliced
100 g/3½ oz fresh or
   frozen green peas
chopped fresh mint or
   coriander leaves,
   to garnish

❶ Heat the oil in a large saucepan or a cast-iron casserole over a medium–high heat. Add the lamb, in batches if necessary to avoid crowding the pan, and cook until evenly browned on all sides, adding a little more oil if needed. Remove the meat with a slotted spoon when browned.

❷ Reduce the heat and add the onion and garlic to the pan. Cook, stirring frequently, for 1–2 minutes.

❸ Add the water and return all the meat to the pan. Bring just to the boil and skim off any foam that rises to the surface. Reduce the heat and stir in the tomatoes, bay leaf, thyme, oregano, cinnamon, cumin, turmeric and harissa. Simmer for about 1 hour, or until the meat is very tender. Discard the bay leaf.

❹ Stir in the chickpeas, carrot and potato, and simmer for 15 minutes. Add the courgette and peas and continue simmering for 15–20 minutes, or until all the vegetables are tender.

❺ Adjust the seasoning, adding more harissa, if desired. Ladle the soup into warm bowls and garnish with chopped mint or coriander leaves.

easy

serves 4

15–20 minutes

about 2 hours

Turkey Soup with Rice, Mushrooms & Sage

INGREDIENTS

40 g/1½ oz butter
1 onion, chopped finely
1 celery stick, chopped finely
25 large fresh sage leaves, chopped finely
4 tbsp plain flour
1.2 litres/2 pints turkey or chicken stock
100 g/3½ oz brown rice
250 g/9 oz mushrooms, sliced
200 g/7 oz cooked turkey
200 ml/7 fl oz double cream
freshly grated Parmesan cheese, to serve

❶ Melt half the butter in a large saucepan over a medium–low heat. Add the onion, celery and sage, and fry for 3–4 minutes, or until the onion is softened, stirring frequently. Stir in the flour and continue cooking for 2 minutes.

❷ Add about a quarter of the stock a little at a time, and stir well, scraping the bottom of the pan to mix in the flour. Pour in the remaining stock, stirring to combine completely, and bring just to the boil.

❸ Stir in the rice and season to taste. Reduce the heat and simmer gently, partially covered, for about 30 minutes, or until the rice is just tender, stirring occasionally.

❹ Meanwhile, melt the remaining butter in a large frying pan over a medium heat. Add the mushrooms and season with salt and pepper. Cook for about 8 minutes, or until they are golden brown, stirring occasionally at first, then more often after they start to colour. Add the mushrooms to the soup.

❺ Add the turkey to the soup and stir in the cream. Continue simmering for about 10 minutes, or until heated through. Taste and adjust the seasoning, if necessary. Ladle into warm bowls and serve with Parmesan cheese.

very easy

serves 4

10 minutes

about 1 hour

Minestrone

INGREDIENTS

1 tbsp olive oil
1 onion, chopped finely
1 leek, halved lengthways
    and sliced thinly
2 garlic cloves, chopped
    finely
400 g/14 oz canned
    chopped tomatoes
    in juice
1 carrot, diced finely
1 small turnip,
    diced finely
1 small potato,
    diced finely
125 g/4½ oz peeled
    celeriac, diced finely
250 g/9 oz peeled
    pumpkin flesh,
    diced finely
700 ml/1¼ pints water
1 litre/1¾ pints chicken
    or vegetable stock
400 g/14 oz canned
    cannellini or borlotti
    beans, rinsed
100 g/3½ oz leafy
    cabbage
85 g/3 oz pasta shapes
    or broken spaghetti
salt and pepper
freshly grated Parmesan
    cheese, to serve

❶ Heat the oil in a large saucepan over a medium heat. Add the onion, leek and garlic, and fry for 3–4 minutes, stirring occasionally, until slightly softened.

❷ Add the tomatoes, carrot, turnip, potato, celeriac, pumpkin, water and stock. Bring to the boil, stirring the pan occasionally.

❸ Stir in the beans and cabbage. Season lightly with salt and pepper. Reduce the heat and simmer, partially covered, for about 50 minutes, or until all the vegetables are tender.

❹ Bring salted water to the boil in a saucepan. Add the pasta and cook until it is just tender. Drain and add the pasta to the soup.

❺ Taste the soup and adjust the seasoning. Ladle into warm bowls and serve hot with freshly grated Parmesan cheese to sprinkle on top.

 extremely easy

serves 4

20 minutes

1 hour,
10 minutes

Vegetable Chilli

INGREDIENTS

1 medium aubergine,
   peeled if wished, cut
   into 2.5 cm/1 inch
   slices
1 tbsp olive oil, plus extra
   for brushing
1 large red or yellow
   onion, chopped finely
2 peppers, chopped
   finely
3–4 garlic cloves,
   chopped finely or
   crushed
800 g/28 oz canned
   chopped tomatoes
   in juice
1 tbsp mild chilli powder,
   or to taste
½ tsp ground cumin
½ tsp dried oregano
2 small courgettes,
   quartered lengthways
   and sliced
400 g/14 oz canned
   kidney beans,
   drained and rinsed
450 ml/16 fl oz water
1 tbsp tomato purée
6 spring onions,
   chopped finely
115 g/4 oz grated
   Cheddar cheese
salt and pepper

easy

serves 4

15 minutes

1 hour,
25 minutes

❶ Brush the aubergine slices on one side with olive oil. Heat half the oil in a large frying pan over a medium–high heat. Add the aubergine, oiled side up, and cook for 5–6 minutes, or until browned on one side. Turn, brown the other side, transfer to a plate, and cut into bite-sized pieces.

❷ Heat the remaining oil in a large saucepan over a medium heat. Add the onion and peppers, cover, and cook for 3–4 minutes, stirring occasionally, until the onion is just softened. Add the garlic and continue cooking for 2–3 minutes, or until the onion begins to colour.

❸ Add the tomatoes, chilli powder, cumin and oregano. Season with salt and pepper. Bring just to the boil, reduce the heat, cover, and simmer for 15 minutes.

❹ Add the courgettes, aubergine pieces and beans. Stir in the water and the tomato purée. Cover again and continue simmering for about 45 minutes, or until the vegetables are tender. Taste and adjust the seasoning. If you prefer a spicier chilli, stir in a little more chilli powder.

❺ Season to taste. Ladle the chilli into bowls and top with spring onions and grated cheese.

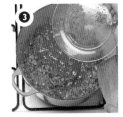

Mushroom & Barley Soup

INGREDIENTS

60 g/2¼ oz pearl barley
1.5 litres/2¾ pints
  chicken or vegetable
  stock
1 bay leaf
1 tbsp butter
350 g/12 oz mushrooms,
  sliced thinly
1 tsp olive oil
1 onion, chopped finely
2 carrots, sliced thinly
1 tbsp chopped fresh
  tarragon
1 tbsp chopped fresh
  parsley or tarragon,
  to garnish

❶ Rinse the barley and drain. Bring 450 ml/16 fl oz of the stock to the boil in a small saucepan. Add the bay leaf and, if the stock is unsalted, add a large pinch of salt. Stir in the barley, reduce the heat, cover, and simmer for 40 minutes.

❷ Melt the butter in a large frying pan over a medium heat. Add the mushrooms and season with salt and pepper. Cook for about 8 minutes, or until they are golden brown, stirring occasionally at first, then more often after they start to colour. Remove the mushrooms from the heat.

❸ Heat the oil in a large saucepan over a medium heat and add the onion and carrots. Cover and cook for about 3 minutes, stirring frequently, until the onion is softened.

❹ Add the remaining stock and bring to the boil. Stir in the barley with its cooking liquid, and add the mushrooms. Reduce the heat, cover, and simmer the soup gently for about 20 minutes, or until the carrots are tender, stirring the pan occasionally.

❺ Stir in the chopped tarragon. Taste and adjust the seasoning, if necessary. Ladle into warm bowls, then garnish with fresh parsley or tarragon, and serve.

very easy

serves 4

10 minutes

1¼ hours

Vegetable Soup with Bulgar Wheat & Herbs

INGREDIENTS

1 tbsp olive oil
2 onions, chopped
3 garlic cloves, chopped finely or crushed
50 g/1¾ oz bulgar wheat
5 tomatoes, skinned and sliced, or 400 g/14 oz canned plum tomatoes in juice
225 g/8 oz peeled pumpkin or acorn squash, diced
1 large courgette, quartered lengthways and sliced
1 litre/1¾ pints boiling water
2 tbsp tomato purée
¼ tsp chilli purée
40 g/1½ oz chopped mixed fresh oregano, basil and flat-leaved parsley
25 g/1 oz rocket leaves, chopped coarsely
175 g/6 oz shelled fresh or frozen peas
salt and pepper
freshly grated Parmesan cheese, to serve

❶ Heat the oil in a large saucepan over a medium–low heat and add the onions and garlic. Cover and fry for 5–8 minutes, or until the onions soften.

❷ Stir in the bulgar wheat and continue cooking for 1 minute.

❸ Layer the tomatoes, pumpkin or squash and courgette in the saucepan.

❹ Combine half the water with the tomato purée, chilli purée and a large pinch of salt. Pour the liquid over the vegetables. Cover the pan, and simmer for 15 minutes.

❺ Uncover the saucepan and stir. Put all the herbs and the rocket on top of the soup, and layer the peas over them. Pour the remaining water into the pan and bring to the boil gently. Reduce the heat and simmer for 20–25 minutes, or until all the vegetables are tender.

❻ Stir the soup. Taste and adjust the seasoning, adding salt and pepper if necessary, and a little more chilli purée to taste. Ladle the soup into warm bowls and serve with Parmesan cheese.

easy

serves 4

10 minutes

1 hour

Main
Meals

As these dishes are cooked in just one pot, all the goodness and flavour of the ingredients are cooked into the soup. Simmered Stew of Meat, Chicken, Vegetables & Fruit is a dish that contains proteins and vitamins, and its fruit gives it an intriguing taste and texture. The classic stews such as Lamb Hotpot and the wonderful Maltese Rabbit with Fennel can be left unattended to simmer slowly. By contrast, Stir-fried Squid with Hot Black Bean Sauce takes only minutes to toss in a wok. This Eastern cooking method is not only fast but also healthy and versatile.

Osso Bucco with Citrus Rinds

INGREDIENTS

1–2 tbsp plain flour
6 meaty slices osso bucco (veal shins)
1 kg/2 lb 4 oz fresh tomatoes, skinned, deseeded and diced, or 800 g/28 oz canned chopped tomatoes
1–2 tbsp olive oil
250 g/9 oz onions, chopped very finely
250 g/9 oz carrots, diced finely
225 ml/8 fl oz dry white wine
225 ml/8 fl oz veal stock
6 large basil leaves
1 large garlic clove, chopped very finely
finely grated rind of 1 large lemon
finely grated rind of 1 orange
2 tbsp chopped finely fresh flat-leaved parsley
salt and pepper

❶ Put the flour in a plastic bag and season with salt and pepper. Add the osso bucco, a couple of pieces at a time, and shake until well coated. Remove and shake off the excess flour. Continue until all the pieces are coated.

❷ If using canned tomatoes, put them in a sieve and leave to drain.

❸ Heat 1 tablespoon of the oil in a large flameproof casserole. Add the osso bucco and fry for 10 minutes on each side until well browned. Remove from the casserole.

❹ Add 1–2 teaspoons of oil to the casserole if necessary. Add the onions and fry for about 5 minutes, stirring, until soft. Stir in the carrots and fry until they become soft.

❺ Add the tomatoes, wine, stock and basil, and return the osso bucco to the pan. Bring to the boil, then lower the heat and simmer for 1 hour, covered. Check with the tip of a knife that the meat is tender. If not, continue cooking for 10 minutes and test again. When the meat is tender, sprinkle with the garlic and lemon and orange rind. Re-cover and cook for another 10 minutes.

❻ Adjust the seasoning if necessary. Sprinkle with the parsley, and serve.

easy

serves 4

20 minutes

1¾ hours

Spanish Chicken with Garlic

INGREDIENTS

2–3 tbsp plain flour
cayenne pepper
4 chicken quarters
   or other joints,
   patted dry
about 4 tbsp olive oil
20 large garlic cloves,
   each halved and
   green core removed
1 large bay leaf
450 ml/16 fl oz chicken
   stock
4 tbsp dry white wine
chopped fresh parsley,
   to garnish
salt and pepper

❶ Put about 2 tablespoons of the flour in a bag and season to taste with cayenne pepper and salt and pepper. Add a chicken piece and shake until it is lightly coated with the flour, shaking off the excess. Repeat with the remaining pieces, adding more flour and seasoning, if necessary.

❷ Heat 3 tablespoons of the olive oil in a large frying pan. Add the garlic cloves and fry for about 2 minutes, stirring, to flavour the oil. Remove with a slotted spoon and set aside.

❸ Add the chicken to the pan, skin-side down, and fry for 5 minutes, or until golden brown. Turn and fry for another 5 minutes, adding an extra 1–2 tablespoons of oil if needed.

❹ Return the garlic to the pan. Add the bay leaf, chicken stock and wine, and bring to the boil. Lower the heat, cover, and simmer for 25 minutes, or until the chicken is tender and the garlic cloves are very soft. Using a slotted spoon, transfer the chicken to a serving plate and keep warm. Bring the cooking liquid to the boil, with the garlic, and boil until reduced to about 250 ml/9 fl oz. Adjust the seasoning, if necessary.

❺ Spoon the sauce over the chicken pieces and scatter the garlic cloves around. Garnish with parsley and serve.

very easy

serves 4

10 minutes

1 hour

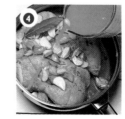
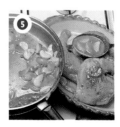

Basque Pork & Beans

INGREDIENTS

200 g/7 oz dried
  cannellini beans,
  soaked overnight
olive oil
600 g/1 lb 5 oz boneless
  leg of pork, cut into
  5 cm/2 inch chunks
1 large onion, sliced
3 large garlic cloves,
  crushed
400 g/14 oz canned
  chopped tomatoes
2 green peppers, cored,
  deseeded and sliced
finely grated rind of
  1 large orange
salt and pepper
finely chopped fresh
  parsley, to garnish

❶ Drain the cannellini beans and put in a large saucepan with fresh water to cover. Bring to the boil and cook rapidly for 10 minutes. Lower the heat and simmer for 20 minutes. Drain and set aside.

❷ Add enough oil to cover the base of a frying pan in a very thin layer. Heat the oil over medium heat, add a few pieces of the pork, and fry on all sides until brown. Repeat with the remaining pork and set aside.

❸ Add 1 tablespoon of oil to the frying pan, if necessary, then add the onion and fry for 3 minutes. Stir in the garlic and fry for another 2 minutes. Return the pork to the pan.

❹ Add the tomatoes to the pan and bring to the boil. Lower the heat, stir in the pepper slices, orange rind, the drained beans, and add salt and pepper to taste.

❺ Transfer the contents of the pan to a casserole dish.

❻ Cover the casserole dish and cook in a preheated oven at 180°C/350°F/Gas Mark 4 for 45 minutes, or until the beans and pork are tender. Sprinkle with parsley and serve.

very easy

serves 4

15 minutes

1 hour,
20 minutes

Maltese Rabbit with Fennel

INGREDIENTS

5 tbsp olive oil
2 large fennel bulbs,
   trimmed and sliced
2 carrots, diced
1 large garlic clove,
   crushed
1 tbsp fennel seeds
about 4 tbsp plain flour
2 wild rabbits, jointed
225 ml/8 fl oz dry
   white wine
225 ml/8 fl oz water
1 bouquet garni of
   2 sprigs fresh flat-
   leaved parsley, 1 sprig
   fresh rosemary and
   1 bay leaf, tied in a
   7.5 cm/3 inch piece
   of celery
salt and pepper
thick, crusty bread,
   to serve

TO GARNISH
finely chopped fresh
   flat-leaved parsley
   or coriander
fresh rosemary sprigs

❶ Heat 3 tablespoons of the olive oil in a large flameproof casserole. Add the fennel and carrots, and fry for 5 minutes, stirring occasionally. Stir in the garlic and fennel seeds and fry for 2 minutes, or until the fennel is tender. Remove the fennel and carrots from the casserole and set aside.

❷ Put 4 tablespoons of flour in a plastic bag, and add seasoning. Add 2 rabbit pieces and shake to coat lightly, then shake off any excess flour. Continue until all the pieces of rabbit are coated, adding more flour if necessary.

❸ Add the remaining oil to the casserole. Fry the rabbit pieces for about 5 minutes on each side until golden brown, working in batches. Remove the rabbit from the casserole as it cooks.

❹ Pour in the wine and bubble over the heat, stirring to scrape up all the bits from the bottom. Return the rabbit pieces, fennel and carrots to the casserole, and pour in the water. Add the bouquet garni and salt and pepper to taste.

❺ Bring to the boil. Lower the heat, cover, and simmer for about 1¼ hours, or until the rabbit is tender.

❻ Discard the bouquet garni. Garnish with herbs and serve straight from the casserole with plenty of bread.

easy

serves 4

15 minutes

1¾ hours

Chicken Basquaise

very easy

serves 4

10 minutes

1½ hours

❶ Dry the chicken pieces well with kitchen paper. Put about 2 tablespoons of flour in a plastic bag, season with salt and pepper and add the chicken pieces. Seal the bag and shake to coat the chicken.

❷ Heat 2 tablespoons of the oil in a large flameproof casserole over a medium–high heat. Add the chicken and fry for about 15 minutes, or until well browned. Transfer to a plate.

❸ Heat the remaining oil in the pan and add the onion and peppers. Reduce the heat to medium and stir-fry until they begin to colour and soften. Add the garlic, chorizo and tomato purée, and continue stirring for about 3 minutes. Add the rice and cook for about 2 minutes, stirring to coat, until the rice is translucent.

❹ Add the stock, crushed chillies, thyme and salt and pepper, and stir. Bring to the boil. Return the chicken to the pan, pressing gently into the rice. Cover and cook over a very low heat for about 45 minutes, or until the chicken and rice are tender.

❺ Gently stir the ham, black olives and half the parsley into the rice mixture. Re-cover and heat through for another 5 minutes. Sprinkle with the remaining parsley and serve.

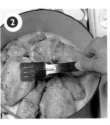
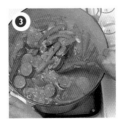

Azerbaijani Lamb Pilaf

INGREDIENTS

2–3 tbsp oil

650 g/1 lb 7 oz boneless
lamb shoulder, cut
into 2.5 cm/1 inch
cubes

2 onions, chopped
coarsely

1 tsp ground cumin

200 g/7 oz arborio,
long-grain or
basmati rice

1 tbsp tomato purée

1 tsp saffron threads

100 ml/3½ fl oz
pomegranate juice

850 ml/1½ pints lamb
or chicken stock,
or water

115 g/4 oz dried apricots
or prunes, ready
soaked and halved

2 tbsp raisins

salt and pepper

TO SERVE

2 tbsp chopped
fresh mint

2 tbsp chopped fresh
watercress

❶ Heat the oil in a large flameproof casserole or a wide saucepan over a high heat. Add the lamb in batches and fry for about 7 minutes, turning, until lightly browned.

❷ Add the onions to the casserole, reduce the heat to medium–high, and fry for about 2 minutes, or until they begin to soften. Add the cumin and rice and cook for about 2 minutes, stirring to coat well, until the rice is translucent. Stir in the tomato purée and the saffron threads.

❸ Add the pomegranate juice and stock, and bring to the boil, stirring once or twice. Add the apricots or prunes and raisins to the casserole, and stir well to combine them. Reduce the heat to low, cover the casserole, and simmer for 20–25 minutes, or until the lamb and rice are tender and the liquid is absorbed.

❹ To serve, sprinkle the chopped mint and watercress over the pilaf and serve hot, straight from the pan.

 very easy

 serves 4

 10 minutes

about 1 hour

Louisiana 'Dirty' Rice

INGREDIENTS

175 g/6 oz belly pork,
  diced, or bacon,
  thickly sliced
225 g/8 oz chicken
  livers, trimmed,
  rinsed, dried and
  chopped
225 g/8 oz chicken
  gizzards, trimmed,
  rinsed, dried and
  chopped finely
1 onion, chopped finely
1 celery stick, chopped
  finely
1 green pepper, cored,
  deseeded and
  chopped
3–4 garlic cloves,
  chopped finely
1 tsp ground cumin
1 tsp hot red pepper
  sauce, or to taste
200 g/7 oz long-grain
  white rice
600 ml/1 pint chicken
  stock
2–3 spring onions, sliced
2–3 tbsp chopped fresh
  flat-leaved parsley
salt and pepper

❶ Fry the pork or bacon in a large heavy-based saucepan for about 7 minutes, or until it is crisp and golden. Using a slotted spoon, remove the pork or bacon to a plate. Add the chicken livers and gizzards and fry, stirring occasionally, for 5 minutes, or until the chicken is tender and lightly golden. Transfer to a plate.

❷ Add the onion, celery and pepper to the pan and fry for about 6 minutes, stirring frequently, until the vegetables are tender. Stir in the garlic, cumin and hot pepper sauce, and cook for another 30 seconds.

❸ Add the rice and cook, stirring, until translucent and well coated with the fat. Add the stock and season with salt and pepper.

❹ Return the cooked bacon, chicken livers and gizzards to the pan, stirring to blend. Cover and simmer gently for 20 minutes, or until the rice is tender and the liquid absorbed.

❺ Fork half the spring onions and the parsley into the rice and toss gently together. Transfer to a serving dish, sprinkle with the remaining spring onions, and serve immediately.

very easy

serves 4

20 minutes

50 minutes

Baked Tomato Rice with Sausages

INGREDIENTS

2 tbsp vegetable oil
1 onion, chopped
   coarsely
1 red pepper, cored,
   deseeded and
   chopped
2 garlic cloves,
   chopped finely
½ tsp dried thyme
300 g/10½ oz long-grain
   white rice
1 litre/1¾ pints light
   chicken or vegetable
   stock
225 g/8 oz canned
   chopped tomatoes
1 bay leaf
2 tbsp shredded
   fresh basil
175 g/6 oz mature
   Cheddar cheese,
   grated
2 tbsp chopped fresh
   chives
4 herby pork sausages,
   cooked and cut into
   1 cm/½ inch pieces
2–3 tbsp freshly grated
   Parmesan cheese

❶ Heat the oil in a large flameproof casserole over a medium heat. Add the onion and red pepper and cook for about 5 minutes, stirring frequently, until the vegetables are soft and lightly coloured. Stir in the garlic and thyme and cook for another minute.

❷ Add the rice and cook, stirring frequently, for about 2 minutes, or until the grains are well coated and translucent. Stir in the stock, tomatoes and bay leaf. Boil for 5 minutes, or until the stock is almost absorbed.

❸ Stir in the basil, Cheddar cheese, chives and pork sausages, and bake, covered, in a preheated oven at 180°C/350°F/Gas Mark 4 for about 25 minutes.

❹ Sprinkle with the Parmesan cheese and return to the oven, uncovered, for 5 minutes, or until the top is golden. Serve hot from the casserole.

extremely easy

serves 4

15 minutes

55 minutes

Creole Jambalaya

INGREDIENTS

2 tbsp vegetable oil
85 g/3 oz piece quality
smoked ham, cubed
85 g/3 oz andouille or
pure smoked pork
sausage, cubed
2 large onions, chopped
3–4 celery sticks, chopped
2 green peppers, cored,
and chopped finely
2 garlic cloves, chopped
225 g/8 oz chicken meat
4 ripe tomatoes, skinned
175 ml/6 fl oz passata
450 ml/16 fl oz fish stock
400 g/14 oz long-grain
white rice
4 spring onions, cut into
2.5 cm/1 inch pieces
250 g/9 oz peeled raw
prawns, tails on
250 g/9 oz cooked white
crab meat
12 oysters, shelled, with
their liquor

SEASONING MIX
2 dried bay leaves
1 tsp salt
1½–2 tsp cayenne pepper
1½ tsp dried oregano
1 tsp white pepper
1 tsp black pepper

easy

serves 4

20 minutes

50 minutes, plus
3 minutes to
stand

❶ To make the seasoning mix, mix the ingredients in a bowl.

❷ Heat the oil in a flameproof casserole over a medium heat. Add the cubes of ham and sausage, and fry, stirring frequently, for about 8 minutes or until golden. Using a slotted spoon, transfer to a large plate.

❸ Add the onions, celery and peppers to the casserole and cook for about 4 minutes, or until just softened. Stir in the garlic, then remove and set aside.

❹ Chop the chicken meat and add to the casserole. Cook for 3–4 minutes, or until they begin to colour. Stir in the seasoning mix to coat them. Return the ham, sausage and vegetables to the casserole and stir to combine. Chop the tomatoes and add them, with the passata, then pour in the stock. Bring to the boil.

❺ Stir in the rice and reduce the heat to a simmer. Cook for about 12 minutes. Uncover, stir in the spring onions and prawns, and cook, covered, for 4 minutes.

❻ Add the crab meat and oysters with their liquor and gently stir in. Cook until the rice is just tender and the oysters are beginning to firm. Remove from the heat and leave to stand, covered, for about 3 minutes before serving.

Spicy Pork with Prunes

INGREDIENTS

1.5 kg/3 lb 5 oz pork
joint, such as leg or
shoulder
juice of 2–3 limes
10 garlic cloves, chopped
3–4 tbsp mild chilli
powder, such as ancho
or New Mexico
4 tbsp vegetable oil
2 onions, chopped
500 ml/18 fl oz chicken
stock
25 small tart tomatoes,
chopped coarsely
25 prunes, stoned
1–2 tsp sugar
about a pinch of
ground cinnamon
about a pinch of
ground allspice
about a pinch of
ground cumin
salt
warmed corn tortillas,
to serve

❶ Combine the pork with the lime juice, garlic, chilli powder, 2 tablespoons of oil, and salt. Leave to marinate in the refrigerator overnight.

❷ Remove the pork from the marinade. Wipe it dry with kitchen paper and reserve the marinade. Heat the remaining oil in a flameproof casserole and brown the pork evenly until just golden. Add the onions, the reserved marinade, and the stock. Cover and cook in a preheated oven at 180°C/350°F/ Gas Mark 4 for 2–3 hours, or until tender.

❸ Spoon any fat from the surface of the cooking liquid and add the tomatoes. Continue to cook for about 20 minutes, or until the tomatoes are tender. Mash the tomatoes into a coarse purée. Add the prunes and sugar, then adjust the seasoning, adding cinnamon, allspice and cumin, and extra chilli powder, to taste.

❹ Increase the temperature of the oven to 200°C/400°F/ Gas Mark 6 and return the meat and sauce to the oven for another 20–30 minutes, or until the meat has browned on top and the juices have thickened.

❺ Remove the meat from the pan and leave it to stand for a few minutes. Carefully carve it into thin slices and spoon the sauce over the top. Serve warm, with corn tortillas.

easy

serves 4

15 minutes,
plus 12 hours
to marinate

4 hours

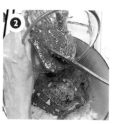

Simmered Stew of Meat, Chicken, Vegetables & Fruit

INGREDIENTS

900 g / 2 lb boneless
  pork, either in one
  joint or in pieces
2 bay leaves
1 onion, chopped
8 garlic cloves, chopped
2 tbsp chopped fresh
  coriander
1 carrot, sliced thinly
2 celery sticks, diced
2 chicken stock cubes
½ chicken, cut into
  portions
4–5 ripe tomatoes, diced
½ tsp mild chilli powder
grated rind of ¼ orange
¼ tsp ground cumin
juice of 3 oranges
1 courgette, cut into bite-
  sized pieces
¼ cabbage, sliced thinly
  and blanched
1 apple, cut into pieces
about 10 prunes, stoned
¼ tsp ground cinnamon
pinch of dried ginger
2 hard chorizo sausages,
  about 350 g / 12 oz in
  total, cut into pieces
salt and pepper

❶ Combine the pork, bay leaves, onion, garlic, coriander, carrot and celery in a large saucepan and fill with cold water. Bring to the boil, then skim off the scum from the surface. Reduce the heat and simmer gently for 1 hour.

❷ Add the stock cubes to the pan with the chicken and tomatoes, and the chilli powder, orange rind and cumin. Cook for another 45 minutes, or until the chicken is tender. Spoon off the fat that forms on the top of the liquid.

❸ Add the orange juice, chopped courgette, cabbage, apple, prunes, cinnamon, ginger and chorizo. Continue to simmer for another 20 minutes, or until the courgette pieces are soft and tender and the chorizo is cooked.

❹ Season the stew with salt and pepper to taste. Serve immediately.

extremely easy

serves 4

20 minutes

2 hours,
20 minutes

Potato, Beef & Peanut Pot

INGREDIENTS

1 tbsp vegetable oil
60 g/2¼ oz butter
450 g/1 lb beef steak
1 onion, sliced
2 garlic cloves, crushed
2 large waxy potatoes,
  cubed
½ tsp paprika
4 tbsp crunchy peanut
  butter
600 ml/1 pint beef stock
25 g/1 oz unsalted
  peanuts
2 tsp light soy sauce
50 g/1¾ oz sugar snap
  peas
1 red pepper, cut into
  strips
parsley sprigs, to garnish

 extremely easy

 serves 4

10 minutes

1 hour,
10 minutes

❶ Heat the oil and butter in a flameproof casserole dish.

❷ Cut the beef into strips, put them in the dish, and fry them gently for 3–4 minutes, stirring and turning the meat until it is sealed on all sides.

❸ Add the onion and garlic and fry for another 2 minutes, stirring constantly.

❹ Add the potato cubes and fry for 3–4 minutes, or until they begin to brown slightly.

❺ Stir in the paprika and peanut butter, then blend in the beef stock a little at a time. Bring the mixture to the boil, stirring frequently.

❻ Add the peanuts, soy sauce, sugar snap peas and pepper.

❼ Cover and cook over a low heat for 45 minutes, or until the beef is cooked through. Garnish the dish with parsley sprigs, if wished, and serve hot.

COOK'S TIP
Add a chopped green chilli to the sauce for extra spice.

Lamb Hotpot

INGREDIENTS

675 g/1½ lb best end of
   lamb neck cutlets
2 lamb's kidneys
675 g/1½ lb waxy
   potatoes, scrubbed
   and sliced thinly
1 large onion,
   sliced thinly
2 tbsp chopped
   fresh thyme
150 ml/5 fl oz lamb stock
25 g/1 oz butter, melted
salt and pepper
fresh thyme sprigs,
   to garnish

❶ Remove any excess fat from the lamb. Skin and core the kidneys and cut them into slices.

❷ Arrange a thick layer of potatoes in the base of a 1.7 litre/3 pint ovenproof dish.

❸ Arrange the lamb neck cutlets on top of the potatoes and cover with the sliced kidneys, onion and chopped fresh thyme.

❹ Pour the lamb stock over the meat and season to taste with salt and pepper.

❺ Layer the remaining potato slices on top, overlapping them to cover the meat and sliced onion completely.

❻ Brush the potato slices with the butter, cover the dish, and cook in a preheated oven, 180°C/350°F/Gas Mark 4, for 1½ hours.

extremely easy

serves 4

15 minutes

2 hours

❼ Remove the lid and cook for another 30 minutes, or until golden brown on top.

❽ Garnish with fresh thyme sprigs and serve hot.

COOK'S TIP
Although this is a classic recipe, extra ingredients of your choice, such as celery or carrots, can be added to the dish for variety and colour.

❶ 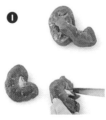 ❷  ❺

Country Braised Chicken & Rosemary Dumplings

INGREDIENTS

4 chicken quarters
2 tbsp sunflower oil
2 medium leeks
250 g/9 oz carrots,
    chopped
250 g/9 oz parsnips,
    chopped
2 small turnips, chopped
600 ml/1 pint chicken
    stock
3 tbsp Worcestershire
    sauce
2 sprigs fresh rosemary
salt and pepper

DUMPLINGS
200 g/7 oz self-raising
    flour
100 g/3½ oz shredded
    suet
1 tbsp chopped
    rosemary leaves
cold water, to mix

❶ Remove the skin from the chicken if you prefer. Heat the oil in a large, flameproof casserole or a heavy saucepan, and fry the chicken until golden. Using a slotted spoon, remove the chicken from the pan. Drain off the excess fat.

❷ Trim and slice the leeks. Add the carrots, parsnips and turnips to the casserole and cook for 5 minutes, or until lightly coloured. Return the chicken to the pan.

❸ Add the chicken stock, Worcestershire sauce, rosemary and seasoning, then bring to the boil.

❹ Reduce the heat, cover the pan, and simmer gently for about 50 minutes, or until the juices run clear when the chicken is pierced with a skewer.

❺ To make the dumplings, combine the flour, suet and rosemary leaves with salt and pepper in a bowl. Stir in just enough cold water to bind to a firm dough.

❻ Form into 8 small balls and place them on top of the chicken and vegetables. Cover and simmer for another 10–12 minutes, or until the dumplings are well risen. Serve with the casserole.

easy

serves 4

15 minutes

1 hour,
20 minutes

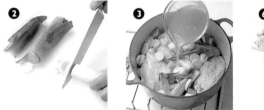

Seafood Stew

INGREDIENTS

225 g/8 oz clams
700 g/1 lb 9 oz mixed
    fish, such as sea bass,
    skate, red snapper,
    rock fish and any
    Mediterranean fish
    you can find
12–18 tiger prawns
about 3 tbsp olive oil
1 large onion,
    chopped finely
2 garlic cloves,
    chopped very finely
2 sun-ripened tomatoes,
    halved, deseeded
    and chopped
700 ml/1¼ pints good-
    quality, ready-made
    chilled fish stock
1 tbsp tomato purée
1 tsp fresh thyme leaves
pinch of saffron threads
pinch of sugar
salt and pepper
finely chopped fresh
    parsley, to garnish

❶ Leave the clams to soak in a bowl of lightly salted water for 30 minutes. Rinse them under cold, running water and scrub lightly to remove any sand from the shells. Discard any broken clams or open clams that do not shut when tapped firmly with the back of a knife, since these will be unsafe to eat.

❷ Prepare the fish as necessary, removing any skin and bones, then cut into bite-sized chunks. To prepare the prawns, break off the heads. Peel off the shells, leaving the tails intact, if wished. Using a small knife, make a slit along the back of each and remove the thin black vein. Set all the seafood aside.

❸ Heat the oil in a large saucepan. Add the onion and fry for 5 minutes, stirring. Add the garlic and fry for another 2 minutes, or until the onion is soft, but not brown.

❹ Add the tomatoes, stock, tomato purée, thyme leaves, saffron threads and sugar, then bring to the boil, stirring to dissolve the tomato purée. Lower the heat, cover, and simmer for 15 minutes. Adjust the seasoning.

❺ Add the seafood and simmer until the clams open and the fish flakes easily. Discard any clams that do not open. Garnish with parsley and serve at once.

easy

serves 4

25 minutes,
plus 30 minutes
to soak

35 minutes

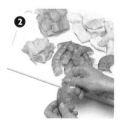

Mediterranean Monkfish

600 g/1 lb 5 oz vine-ripened cherry tomatoes, a mixture of yellow and red, if available
2 monkfish fillets, about 350 g/12 oz each
8 tbsp pesto sauce
salt and pepper
fresh basil sprigs, to garnish

very easy

serves 4

15 minutes

16–18 minutes

❶ Cut the tomatoes in half and scatter, cut-sides up, on the base of an ovenproof serving dish. Set aside.

❷ Using your fingers, rub off the thin grey membrane that covers the monkfish.

❸ If the skin has not been removed, place the fish skin-side down on the work surface. Loosen enough skin at one end of the fillet so you can grip hold of it. Work from the front of the fillet to the back. Insert the knife, almost flat, and using a gentle sawing action, remove the skin. Rinse the fillets well and dry with kitchen paper.

❹ Place the fillets on top of the tomatoes, tucking the thin end under, if necessary (see Cook's Tip). Spread 4 tablespoons of the pesto sauce over each fillet and season with pepper.

❺ Cover the dish tightly with foil, shiny-side down. Place in a preheated oven at 230°C/450°F/Gas Mark 8 and roast for 16–18 minutes, or until the fish is cooked through, the flesh flakes easily, and the tomatoes are dissolving into a thick sauce.

❻ Adjust the seasoning, if necessary. Garnish with basil sprigs and serve at once with new potatoes.

COOK'S TIP
Monkfish fillets are often cut from the tail, so the tail end is thinnest end and easily overcooked. Fold the thin end under for even cooking.

Moules Marinara

*2 kg/4 lb 8 oz live
    mussels*
4 tbsp olive oil
*4–6 large garlic cloves,
    halved*
*800 g/28 oz canned
    chopped tomatoes*
*300 ml/10 fl oz dry
    white wine*
*2 tbsp finely chopped
    fresh flat-leaved
    parsley, plus extra
    for garnishing*
*1 tbsp finely chopped
    fresh oregano*
salt and pepper
French bread, to serve

❶ Leave the mussels to soak in a bowl of lightly salted water for 30 minutes. Rinse them under cold, running water and lightly scrub to remove any sand from the shells. Using a small sharp knife, remove the beards from the shells.

❷ Discard any broken mussels or open mussels that do not shut when firmly tapped with the back of a knife — these will be unsafe to eat. Rinse the mussels again, then set aside in a colander.

❸ Heat the olive oil in a saucepan or a stockpot, then add the garlic and fry, stirring, for about 3 minutes to flavour the oil. Using a slotted spoon, remove the garlic from the pan.

❹ Add the tomatoes and their juice, the wine, parsley and oregano, and bring to the boil, stirring. Lower the heat, cover, and simmer for 5 minutes to allow the flavours to blend. Add the mussels, cover the pan, and simmer for 5–8 minutes, shaking the pan regularly, until the mussels open. Using a slotted spoon, transfer the mussels to serving bowls, discarding any that are not open.

❺ Season the sauce to taste. Ladle the sauce over the mussels, sprinkle with extra chopped parsley, and serve at once with plenty of French bread.

easy

serves 4

15 minutes, plus 30 minutes to soak

about 25 minutes

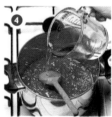

Spicy Coconut Rice with Monkfish & Peas

INGREDIENTS

1 hot red chilli, deseeded and chopped
1 tsp crushed chilli flakes
2 garlic cloves, chopped
2 pinches saffron
3 tbsp coarsely chopped mint leaves
4 tbsp olive oil
2 tbsp lemon juice
350 g/12 oz monkfish fillet, cut into bite-sized pieces
1 onion, chopped finely
400 g/14 oz long-grain rice
400 g/14 oz canned chopped tomatoes
200 ml/7 fl oz coconut milk
115 g/4 oz peas
salt and pepper
2 tbsp chopped coriander, to garnish

❶ In a food processor or a blender, blend together the fresh and dried chilli, garlic, saffron, mint, olive oil and lemon juice until chopped finely, but not smooth.

❷ Put the monkfish into a nonmetal dish and pour the spice paste over it, mixing together well. Set aside for 20 minutes to marinate.

❸ Heat a saucepan until very hot. Using a slotted spoon, lift the monkfish from the marinade and add in batches to the hot pan. Cook for 3–4 minutes, or until browned and firm. Remove with a slotted spoon and set aside.

❹ Add the onion and marinade to the pan and cook for 5 minutes, until the onion is softened. Add the rice and stir until well coated. Add the tomatoes and coconut milk. Bring to the boil, cover, and simmer gently for 15 minutes. Stir in the peas, season, and arrange the fish over the top.

❺ Cover with foil and continue to cook over a very low heat for 5 minutes. Serve garnished with the chopped coriander.

very easy

serves 4

15 minutes, plus 20 minutes to marinate

35 minutes

Stir-fried Squid with Hot Black Bean Sauce

INGREDIENTS

750 g/1 lb 10 oz squid,
   cleaned
1 large red pepper,
   deseeded
85 g/3 oz mangetouts,
   trimmed
1 head pak choi
3 tbsp black bean sauce
1 tbsp Thai fish sauce
1 tbsp rice wine
1 tbsp dark soy sauce
1 tsp soft light brown
   sugar
1 tsp cornflour
1 tbsp water
1 tbsp sunflower oil
1 tsp sesame oil
1 small red bird's eye
   chilli, chopped
1 garlic clove, chopped
   finely
1 tsp fresh ginger root,
   grated
2 spring onions,
   chopped

❶ Cut the tentacles from the squid and discard. Cut the body cavities into quarters lengthways. Use the tip of a small sharp knife to score a diamond pattern into the flesh, without cutting all the way through. Pat dry with kitchen paper.

❷ Cut the pepper into long, thin slices. Cut the mangetouts in half diagonally. Shred the pak choi coarsely.

❸ Mix together the black bean sauce, fish sauce, rice wine, soy sauce and sugar. Blend the cornflour with the water and stir into the other sauce ingredients. Keep to one side.

❹ Heat the oils in a wok. Add the chilli, garlic, ginger and spring onions, and stir-fry for about 1 minute. Add the pepper and stir-fry for about 2 minutes.

❺ Add the squid and stir-fry over a high heat for another minute. Stir in the mangetouts and pak choi, and stir for another minute, or until wilted.

❻ Stir in the sauce ingredients and cook, stirring, for about 2 minutes, or until the sauce clears and thickens. Serve the stir-fry immediately, straight from the pan.

easy

serves 4

20 minutes

10 minutes

Rice with Seafood

INGREDIENTS

12 mussels in shells,
  cleaned
2 litres / 3½ pints fish
  stock
2 tbsp vegetable oil
1 garlic clove, crushed
1 tsp fresh ginger root,
  grated
1 red bird's eye chilli,
  chopped
2 spring onions,
  chopped
225 g / 8 oz long-grain
  rice
2 small squid, cleaned
  and sliced
100 g / 3½ oz firm white
  fish fillet, such as
  halibut or monkfish,
  cut into chunks
100 g / 3½ oz raw prawns,
  peeled
2 tbsp Thai fish sauce
3 tbsp fresh coriander,
  shredded

❶ Discard any mussels with damaged shells or open ones that do not close when tapped firmly. Heat 4 tablespoons of the stock in a large pan. Add the mussels, cover, and shake the pan until the mussels open. Remove from the heat and discard any which do not open.

❷ Heat the oil in a large frying pan or a wok and fry the garlic, ginger, chilli and spring onions for 30 seconds. Add the stock and bring to the boil.

❸ Stir in the rice, then add the squid, fish fillet and prawns. Lower the heat and simmer gently for 15 minutes, or until the rice is cooked. Add the fish sauce and the mussels.

❹ Ladle into wide bowls and sprinkle with coriander, and serve immediately, while hot.

easy

serves 4

15 minutes

20 minutes

Pasta Parcels

INGREDIENTS

*450 g/1 lb dried
   fettuccine*
*150 ml/5 fl oz pesto
   sauce*
4 tsp extra virgin olive oil
*750 g/1 lb 10 oz large
   raw prawns, peeled
   and deveined*
2 garlic cloves, crushed
*125 ml/4 fl oz dry
   white wine*
salt and pepper

❶ Cut out 4 x 30 cm/12 inch squares of greaseproof paper.

❷ Bring a large saucepan of lightly salted water to the boil. Add the fettuccine and cook for 2–3 minutes, or until just softened. Drain and set aside.

❸ Mix together the fettuccine and half of the pesto sauce. Spread out the paper squares and put 1 teaspoon olive oil in the middle of each. Divide the fettuccine between the squares, then divide the prawns and place them on top of the fettuccine.

❹ Mix together the remaining pesto sauce and the garlic and spoon it over the prawns. Season each parcel with salt and black pepper, and sprinkle with the white wine.

❺ Dampen the edges of the greaseproof paper and wrap the parcels loosely, twisting the edges to seal.

❻ Place the parcels on a baking sheet and bake in a preheated oven at 200°C/400°F/Gas Mark 6 for 10–15 minutes. Transfer the parcels to 4 individual serving plates and serve immediately.

easy

serves 4

20 minutes

18 minutes

Spanish Paella

INGREDIENTS

125 ml/4 fl oz olive oil
1.5 kg/3 lb 5 oz chicken,
   cut into 8 pieces
350 g/12 oz chorizo
   sausage, cut into
   1 cm/½ inch pieces
115 g/4 oz cured ham,
   chopped
2 onions, chopped finely
2 red peppers, cut into
   2.5 cm/1 inch pieces
4–6 garlic cloves
750 g/1 lb 10 oz short-
   grain Spanish rice
2 bay leaves
1 tsp dried thyme
1 tsp saffron threads,
   lightly crushed
225 ml/8 fl oz dry
   white wine
1.5 litres/2¾ pints
   chicken stock
115 g/4 oz fresh shelled
   or defrosted peas
450 g/1 lb medium
   uncooked prawns
8 raw king prawns,
   in shells
16 clams, scrubbed
16 mussels, scrubbed
salt and pepper
4 tbsp chopped fresh
   flat-leaved parsley

 easy

serves 4

15 minutes

about 1 hour,
plus 5 minutes
to stand

❶ Heat half the oil in a 46 cm/18 inch paella pan or a deep, wide frying pan, then add the chicken and fry gently, turning, until golden brown. Remove from the pan and set aside. Add the chorizo and ham to the pan and fry for about 7 minutes, stirring occasionally, until crisp. Remove and set aside.

❷ Stir the onions into the pan and cook for about 3 minutes, or until soft. Add the peppers and garlic and cook until they begin to soften. Remove and set aside. Add the remaining oil to the pan and stir in the rice until well coated. Stir in the bay leaves, thyme and saffron. Pour in the wine and allow it to bubble, then pour in the stock and stir well, scraping the bottom of the pan. Bring to the boil, stirring often.

❸ Stir in the chorizo, ham and chicken with the cooked vegetables, and gently bury them in the rice. Reduce the heat and cook for 10 minutes, stirring occasionally.

❹ Add the peas and prawns, and cook for another 5 minutes. Push the clams and mussels into the rice. Cover and cook over a very low heat for about 5 minutes, or until the rice is tender and the shellfish open. Discard any unopened clams or mussels. Season to taste.

❺ Remove from the heat, and stand, covered, for about 5 minutes. Sprinkle with parsley and serve.

Vegetarian Light Meals

A light meal is an appealing alternative to sandwiches for lunch, especially if it can be prepared in one pot. Spaghetti al Tonno is quick, satisfying, and made from ingredients most people keep in store in the kitchen cupboard. Spicy Meat and Chipotle Hash is a Mexican dish taking less than half an hour to prepare and cook. This section is mainly for vegetarians, however. It offers tasty variations on traditional dishes, such as Spicy Potato and Rice Pilaf and Cashew Nut Paella, both easy to cook, colourful and delicious.

Spiced Lentils with Spinach

INGREDIENTS

2 tbsp olive oil
1 large onion, chopped
1 large garlic clove,
  crushed
½ tbsp ground cumin
½ tsp ground ginger
250 g/9 oz Puy lentils
about 600 ml/1 pint
  vegetable or
  chicken stock
100 g/3½ oz baby
  spinach leaves
2 tbsp fresh mint leaves
1 tbsp coriander leaves
1 tbsp flat-leaved parsley
freshly squeezed lemon
  juice
salt and pepper
grated lemon rind,
  to garnish

extremely easy

serves 4

10 minutes

40 minutes

❶ Heat the olive oil in a large frying pan over a medium–high heat. Add the onion and cook for about 6 minutes. Stir in the garlic, cumin and ginger, and continue cooking, stirring occasionally, until the onion just starts to brown.

❷ Stir in the lentils. Pour in enough stock to cover the lentils by 2.5 cm/1 inch and bring to the boil. Lower the heat and simmer for 20 minutes, or according to the instructions on the packet, until the lentils are tender.

❸ Meanwhile, rinse the spinach leaves in several changes of cold water and shake dry. Chop the mint, coriander and parsley leaves finely.

❹ If there is no stock left in the pan, add a little extra. Add the spinach and stir until it begins to wilt. Stir in the mint, coriander and parsley. Adjust the seasoning, adding lemon juice and salt and pepper. Transfer to a serving bowl and serve, garnished with lemon rind.

COOK'S TIP

Green lentils from Puy in France keep their shape even after long cooking. Orange and brown lentils must not be cooked for too long, since they quickly turn to a mush.

Borlotti Beans in Tomato Sauce

INGREDIENTS

600 g/1 lb 5 oz fresh
  borlotti beans,
  in shells
4 large leaves fresh
  sage, torn
1 tbsp olive oil
1 large onion, sliced
  finely
300 ml/10 fl oz good-
  quality bottled tomato
  sauce for pasta
salt and pepper
extra shredded sage
  leaves, to garnish

❶ Shell the borlotti beans. Bring a saucepan of water to the boil, add the beans and torn sage leaves, and simmer for about 12 minutes, or until tender. Drain and set aside.

❷ Heat the oil in a large frying pan over a medium heat. Add the onion and cook, stirring occasionally, for about 5 minutes, or until soft but not brown. Stir the tomato sauce into the pan with the cooked borlotti beans and the torn sage leaves.

❸ Increase the heat and bring to the boil, stirring. Lower the heat, partially cover, and simmer for about 10 minutes, or until the the sauce has reduced slightly.

❹ Adjust the seasoning, transfer to a serving bowl and serve hot, garnished with fresh sage leaves.

extremely easy

serves 4

10 minutes

40 minutes

Fideos Tostados

INGREDIENTS

*350 g/12 oz vermicelli or
angel hair pasta in
coils, roughly broken*
*100 g/3½ oz long-grain
white rice*
*3 tbsp extra-virgin
olive oil*
*200 g/7 oz canned
chopped tomatoes,
drained*
*600 ml/1 pint chicken
stock or water, plus
extra if necessary*
1 bay leaf
*1–2 tsp chopped fresh
oregano or 1 tsp dried
oregano*
½ tsp dried thyme leaves
salt and pepper
*1–2 tbsp sprigs and
chopped fresh
oregano or thyme,
to garnish*

❶ Put the pasta and rice in a dry, large, heavy-based saucepan or a flameproof casserole over a medium–high heat and cook for 5–7 minutes, stirring frequently, until light golden. (The pasta will break unevenly, but this does not matter.)

❷ Stir in 2 tablespoons of the olive oil, together with the chopped tomatoes, stock, bay leaf, oregano and thyme, then season with approximately 1 teaspoon of salt and pepper to taste.

❸ Bring to the boil, reduce the heat to medium, and simmer for about 8 minutes, stirring frequently, to unwind and separate the pasta coils.

❹ Reduce the heat to low and cook, covered, for about 10 minutes, or until the rice and pasta are tender and all the liquid is absorbed. If the rice and pasta are too firm, add about 125 ml/4 fl oz more stock or water and continue to cook, covered, for another 5 minutes. Remove from the heat.

❺ Using a fork, fluff the rice and pasta into a warmed deep serving bowl, and drizzle with the remaining oil. Sprinkle with the herbs and serve immediately.

extremely easy

serves 4

5 minutes

40 minutes

Spicy Potato & Rice Pilaf

INGREDIENTS

200 g/7 oz basmati rice,
   soaked in cold water
   for 20 minutes
2 tbsp vegetable oil
½–¾ tsp cumin seeds
225 g/8 oz potatoes, cut
   into 1 cm/½ inch
   pieces
225 g/8 oz frozen peas,
   defrosted
1 green chilli, deseeded
   and sliced thinly
   (optional)
½ tsp salt
1 tsp garam masala
½ tsp ground turmeric
¼ tsp cayenne pepper
600 ml/1 pint water
2 tbsp chopped fresh
   coriander
1 red onion, chopped
   finely
natural yogurt, to serve

❶ Rinse the soaked rice under cold running water until the water runs clear, drain, and set aside.

❷ Heat the oil in a saucepan, then add the cumin seeds and stir for about 10 seconds, or until the seeds jump and colour.

❸ Add the potatoes, peas and chilli, if using, and stir-fry for 3 minutes, or until the potatoes just begin to soften.

❹ Add the rice and cook, stirring frequently, until well coated. Stir in the salt, garam masala, turmeric and cayenne pepper, then add the water. Bring to the boil, stirring once or twice, then reduce the heat to medium and simmer, covered, until most of the water is absorbed and the surface is filled with little steam-holes. Do not stir.

❺ Reduce the heat to very low and, if possible, raise the pan about 2.5 cm/1 inch above the heat source by resting it on a ring. Cover and steam for another 10 minutes. Remove from the heat, uncover, and cover the rice with kitchen paper or a clean tea towel. Re-cover and leave for 5 minutes.

❻ Fork the rice and potato mixture gently into a warmed serving bowl and sprinkle with the coriander and chopped red onion. Serve hot with yogurt handed round separately.

very easy

serves 4

5 minutes, plus
20 minutes
to soak

30 minutes, plus
5 minutes to stand

Chinese Fried Rice

INGREDIENTS

2–3 tbsp groundnut or
  vegetable oil
2 onions, halved and cut
  lengthways into thin
  wedges
2 garlic cloves,
  sliced thinly
2.5 cm/1 inch piece fresh
  ginger root, peeled,
  sliced and cut into
  slivers
200 g/7 oz cooked ham,
  sliced thinly
750 g/1 lb 10 oz cooked,
  cold long-grain
  white rice
250 g/9 oz cooked
  peeled prawns
115 g/4 oz canned water
  chestnuts, sliced
3 eggs
3 tsp sesame oil
4–6 spring onions,
  diagonally sliced into
  2.5 cm/1 inch pieces
2 tbsp dark soy sauce or
  Thai fish sauce
1 tbsp sweet chilli sauce
2 tbsp chopped fresh
  coriander or flat-
  leaved parsley
salt and pepper

extremely easy

serves 4

15 minutes

10 minutes

❶ Heat 2–3 tablespoons of groundnut oil in a wok or a large, deep frying pan until very hot. Add the onions and stir-fry for about 2 minutes, or until they begin to soften. Add the garlic and ginger, and stir-fry for another minute. Add the ham strips and stir to combine.

❷ Add the cold cooked rice and stir to mix with the vegetables and ham. Stir in the prawns and the water chestnuts. Stir in 2 tablespoons of water and cover the pan quickly. Continue to cook for 2 minutes, shaking the pan occasionally to prevent sticking and to allow the rice to heat through.

❸ Beat the eggs with 1 teaspoon of the sesame oil, and season with salt and pepper. Make a well in the centre of the rice mixture, add the eggs, and begin stirring immediately, gradually drawing the rice into the eggs.

❹ Stir in the spring onions, soy sauce and chilli sauce, and stir-fry. Stir in a little more water if the rice looks dry or is sticking. Drizzle in the remaining sesame oil and stir. Season to taste with salt and pepper.

❺ Remove from the heat, wipe the edge of the wok or frying pan, and sprinkle with the coriander. Serve the fried rice immediately straight from the pan.

Spicy Meat & Chipotle Hash

INGREDIENTS

1 tbsp vegetable oil
1 onion, chopped finely
450 g/1 lb leftover meat,
  such as simmered
  pork or beef, cooled
  and cut into thin strips
1 tbsp mild chilli powder
2 ripe tomatoes,
  deseeded and diced
about 225 ml/8 fl oz
  meat stock
½–1 canned chipotle
  chilli, mashed, plus a
  little of the marinade,
  or a few shakes
  bottled chipotle salsa

TO SERVE
125 ml/4 fl oz soured
  cream
4–6 tbsp chopped fresh
  coriander
4–6 tbsp chopped
  radishes
3–4 leaves crisp lettuce,
  such as cos, shredded
12 corn tortillas

❶ Heat the oil in a frying pan, add the onion, and fry until softened, stirring occasionally. Add the meat and sauté for about 3 minutes, stirring, until lightly browned.

❷ Add the chilli powder, tomatoes and stock, and cook until the tomatoes reduce to a sauce. Mash the meat a little as it cooks.

❸ Add the chipotle chilli and continue to cook and mash until the sauce and meat are nearly blended.

❹ Serve the dish with a stack of warmed corn tortillas so that people can fill them with the meaty mixture to make tacos. Also serve soured cream, fresh coriander, radishes and lettuce for each person to add to the meat.

 extremely easy

serves 4

10 minutes

20 minutes

Cashew Nut Paella

INGREDIENTS

INGREDIENTS

2 tbsp olive oil
1 tbsp butter
1 red onion, chopped
150 g/5½ oz arborio rice
1 tsp ground turmeric
1 tsp ground cumin
½ tsp chilli powder
3 garlic cloves, crushed
1 green chilli, sliced
1 green pepper, diced
1 red pepper, diced
75 g/2¾ oz baby
    sweetcorn, halved
    lengthways
2 tbsp stoned black
    olives
1 large tomato, seeded
    and diced
450 ml/ 16 fl oz
    vegetable stock
75 g/2¾ oz unsalted
    cashew nuts
25 g/1 oz frozen peas
2 tbsp chopped parsley
pinch of cayenne pepper
salt and pepper
fresh herbs, to garnish

❶ Heat the olive oil and butter in a large frying pan or a paella pan until the butter has melted.

❷ Add the chopped onion to the pan and sauté for 2–3 minutes, stirring, until the onion has softened.

❸ Stir in the rice, turmeric, cumin, chilli powder, garlic, chilli, peppers, baby sweetcorn, olives and tomato, and cook over a medium heat for 1–2 minutes, stirring occasionally.

❹ Pour in the stock and bring the mixture to the boil. Reduce the heat and cook for 20 minutes, stirring.

❺ Add the cashew nuts and peas to the mixture in the pan and cook for another 5 minutes, stirring occasionally. Season to taste and sprinkle with parsley and cayenne pepper. Transfer to warm serving plates, garnish, and serve immediately.

very easy

serves 4

15 minutes

40 minutes

Chickpea & Vegetable Casserole

INGREDIENTS

1 tbsp olive oil
1 red onion, halved
   and sliced
3 garlic cloves, crushed
225 g/8 oz spinach
1 fennel bulb,
   cut into eight
1 red pepper, cubed
1 tbsp plain flour
450 ml/ 16 fl oz
   vegetable stock
80 ml/3 fl oz dry
   white wine
400 g/14 oz canned
   chickpeas, drained
1 bay leaf
1 tsp ground coriander
½ tsp paprika
salt and pepper
fennel fronds, to garnish

❶ Heat the olive oil in a large flameproof casserole dish and sauté the onion and garlic for 1 minute, stirring. Add the spinach and cook for 4 minutes, or until wilted.

❷ Add the fennel and pepper and cook for 2 minutes, stirring constantly to coat the ingredients.

❸ Stir in the flour and cook for 1 minute.

❹ Add the stock, wine, chickpeas, bay leaf, coriander and paprika, cover and cook for 30 minutes. Season to taste, garnish with fennel fronds and serve immediately.

extremely easy

serves 4

10 minutes

40 minutes

Spicy Potato & Lemon Casserole

INGREDIENTS

100 ml/3½ fl oz olive oil
2 red onions,
    cut into eight
3 garlic cloves, crushed
2 tsp ground cumin
2 tsp ground coriander
pinch of cayenne pepper
1 carrot, thickly sliced
2 small turnips,
    quartered
1 courgette, sliced
450 g/1 lb potatoes,
    thickly sliced
juice and rind of
    2 large lemons
300 ml/ 10 fl oz
    vegetable stock
2 tbsp chopped
    coriander
salt and pepper

extremely easy

serves 4

15 minutes

about 40 minutes

❶ Heat the olive oil in a flameproof casserole.

❷ Add the red onion and sauté for 3 minutes, stirring.

❸ Add the garlic and cook for 30 seconds. Mix in the spices and cook for 1 minute, stirring.

❹ Add the carrot, turnips, courgette and potatoes, and stir to coat in the oil.

❺ Add the lemon juice and rind, stock, and salt and pepper to taste, cover, and cook the vegetables over a medium heat for 20–30 minutes, stirring occasionally.

❻ Remove the casserole lid, sprinkle in the coriander, and stir well. Serve immediately.

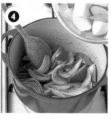

COOK'S TIP

A selection of spices and herbs is important for adding variety to your cooking. Add to your range each time you try a new recipe.

Golden Chicken Risotto

INGREDIENTS

2 tbsp sunflower oil
15 g/½ oz butter or
  margarine
1 medium leek, sliced
  thinly
1 large yellow pepper,
  diced
3 skinless, boneless
  chicken breasts, diced
350 g/12 oz arborio rice
few strands saffron
1.5 litres/2¾ pints
  chicken stock
200 g/7 oz canned
  sweetcorn
60 g/2¼ oz toasted
  unsalted peanuts
60 g/2¼ oz grated
  Parmesan cheese
salt and pepper

❶ Heat the oil and butter or margarine in a large saucepan. Fry the leek and pepper for 1 minute, then stir in the chicken and cook, stirring frequently, until golden brown.

❷ Stir in the rice and cook for 2–3 minutes.

❸ Stir in the saffron strands and add salt and pepper to taste. Add the stock, little by little, cover, and cook over a low heat, stirring occasionally, for 20 minutes, or until the rice is tender and most of the liquid is absorbed. Do not allow the risotto to dry out – add more stock if necessary.

❹ Stir in the sweetcorn, peanuts and Parmesan cheese, then adjust the seasoning to taste. Serve hot.

very easy

serves 4

10 minutes

about 40 minutes

Thai Stir-fried Chicken with Vegetables

INGREDIENTS

3 tbsp sesame oil
350 g/12 oz chicken
    breast, sliced thinly
8 shallots, sliced
2 garlic cloves,
    chopped finely
2.5 cm/1 inch piece fresh
    root ginger, grated
1 green chilli,
    chopped finely
1 each red and green
    pepper, sliced thinly
3 courgettes,
    sliced thinly
2 tbsp ground almonds
1 tsp ground cinnamon
1 tbsp oyster sauce
50 g/1¾ oz creamed
    coconut, grated
salt and pepper

easy

serves 4

20 minutes

10 minutes

❶ Heat the sesame oil in a wok, add the chicken, season with salt and pepper, and stir-fry for about 4 minutes.

❷ Add the shallots, garlic, ginger and chilli, and stir-fry for 2 minutes.

❸ Add the peppers and courgettes and cook for about 1 minute.

❹ Finally, add the remaining ingredients and seasoning. Stir-fry for 1 minute and serve immediately.

COOK'S TIP

Creamed coconut is sold in blocks in supermarkets and Asian stores. It is a useful standby since it adds richness and depth of flavour.

Spaghetti al Tonno

INGREDIENTS

200 g/7 oz canned tuna, drained
60 g/2¼ oz canned anchovies, drained
250 ml/9 fl oz olive oil
60 g/2¼ oz coarsely chopped flat-leaved parsley
150 ml/5 fl oz crème fraîche
450 g/1 lb dried spaghetti
25 g/1 oz butter
salt and pepper
black olives, to garnish
crusty bread, to serve

❶ Remove any bones from the tuna. Put the tuna into a food processor or a blender with the anchovies, 225 ml/ 8 fl oz of the olive oil and the flat-leaved parsley. Process until the sauce is smooth.

❷ Spoon the crème fraîche into the food processor or blender and process again for a few seconds to blend thoroughly. Season to taste with salt and black pepper.

❸ Bring a large pan of lightly salted water to the boil. Add the spaghetti and the remaining olive oil and cook until tender, but still firm to the bite.

❹ Drain the spaghetti, return to the pan, and place it over a medium heat. Add the butter and toss well to coat the pasta well. Spoon in the sauce and quickly toss into the spaghetti using 2 forks.

❺ Remove the pan from the heat and divide the spaghetti between 4 warm individual serving plates. Garnish with the olives and serve immediately with warm, crusty bread.

very easy

serves 4

5 minutes

10–12 minutes